JOB 2.0
GOD AND LUCIFER BATTLE
AGAIN FOR A SINGLE SOUL

JOB 2.0
GOD AND LUCIFER
BATTLE AGAIN FOR A
SINGLE SOUL

Del Staecker

ELM HILL

A Division of
HarperCollins Christian Publishing

www.elmhillbooks.com

JOB 2.0
God and Lucifer battle again for a single soul

Published in Nashville, Tennessee, by Elm Hill, an imprint of Thomas Nelson. Elm Hill and Thomas Nelson are registered trademarks of HarperCollins Christian Publishing, Inc.

Elm Hill titles may be purchased in bulk for educational, business, fund-raising, or sales promotional use. For information, please e-mail SpecialMarkets@ ThomasNelson.com.

Library of Congress Cataloging-in-Publication Data

Library of Congress Control Number: 2019932363

ISBN 978-0-310107583 (Paperback)
ISBN 978-0-310107590 (eBook)

"For it's money they have and peace they lack."

—FIELD OF DREAMS

THE VISIT

O ne day in heaven, while hanging out with his angelic council, God received an unexpected visitor. Actually, the visitor was expected and God knew who was coming. God also knew what was about to happen, which was cool. Surprises were fun, but being the All-Knowing Infinite One, the Creator of Everything Material, Spiritual, and Conscious, could have some drawbacks. You see, for God there were no surprises. God knew everything. It's in his job description.

A second before the visitor knocked at his door, God commanded, "Come in!" Immediately, God said, "Oops!" With a knowing grin, he admitted, "At times I do get ahead of myself." Quickly God focused on the closed door, reversed time, and said, "*Now*, you may come in."

The visitor entered, gazed about Heaven, and cheerfully greeted God with, "Hey, Boss! What's shakin'? Have you created anything new lately?"

It was Lucifer, God's former Number Two.

Lucifer had been out on his own for some time, yet every so often he would drop in for a chat with his former chief. Previously, when he was the highest-ranked member of God's team, Lucifer thought he could run things better than God. In fact, Lucifer believed it so firmly that he even convinced some of his disgruntled teammates to leave Heaven to help him run his own venture—Earth. That was what God had named the spot where he allowed his errant assistant to do "his own thing." As a name, Earth was acceptable for some of its inhabitants, but Lucifer preferred how the Amish so simply and aptly labeled his realm: the Devil's Playground.

When asked to explain his decision to quit God's team and open his own shop, Lucifer would cheekily describe his previous situation in Heaven as "a good position with regular hours and no heavy lifting." If pressed about his departure, Lucifer would share his opinion that "promotion and upward mobility was limited." Always aware of position and status, Lucifer liked to point out his premier leadership position in his new situation. He liked to crow, "Earth is perfect. Here, things are done *my way!*" If seriously pressed about his regular visits to Heaven, Lucifer would slyly admit, "I'd go back permanently, but only if I were the Boss."

Running Earth was indeed a good move for Lucifer. Under his direction it had become "a rockin' place," where promoting and inventing new sins (the stuff not aligned with God) was his primary goal and activity. In the Sin Department, Lucifer was very adept. His motto was: "I'm Good at Being Bad."

On Earth rules were lax and situational ethics prevailed. Most people liked it that way. After Lucifer's involvement in, as he described, "that small incident involving Adam and Eve, which resulted in their departure from Eden," most of humankind gladly accepted his gifts and guidance as the norm. "People love me!" he liked to recount. Yet the fact of the matter was that Lucifer's influence produced much pain and suffering on Earth, and an even greater amount of sadness in Heaven.

Occasionally some thoughtful person on Earth asked why God allowed Evil to go on so freely. God's answer was that it was mankind's choice to listen to and follow Lucifer or not. "People are responsible for their own decisions," he said. Of the few that heard him, they did not like the message. And even fewer chose God's ways over Lucifer's. As noted, God was not happy with the situation. "So many bad choices," he said, aching, "but I love mankind, nonetheless."

Misdirecting people in the daily to and fro of their lives kept Lucifer occupied, but as said, on occasion he would take a break from his mischief and drop in to see his former boss. Lucifer claimed it was for old times' sake, but it was really to keep tabs on his adversary. He pretended to yuck it up with the Boss as a means of gathering useful information to support his various evil doings, and ultimately plot his return. Replacing God was ever in his thoughts. Of course, God was never fooled. You could not fool God.

"How's business?" Lucifer probed with more than a twinkle of mischief in his eyes.

God replied casually, "Same old, same old, you know—infinity in action. Just the usual stuff, I guess."

"Yeah—*you guess*! Like *you don't know*?" quipped Lucifer. He liked to needle God about being the Infinite, All-Knowing, and Eternal Creator.

God grinned just a little at Lucifer's little joke.

"Ha! Gotcha—made you smile!" Lucifer exclaimed as he flashed his trademark luminous smile at the Boss and performed a brief victory dance. Well, it was really just a cute little shuffle step sort of thing.

God grinned a little bit more, holding back his own full smile, which would completely illuminate the Universe. God really liked Lucifer, despite the bad jokes, the rancorous departure, all the efforts to misdirect humankind, and even his plan to take over Heaven. But God did not want to encourage Lucifer's bad behavior. God still had hopes for Lucifer. Even though he was a rotten, evil, duplicitous thief and liar, God still loved Lucifer. God was like that—full of love. In fact, God *is* love—bright, smiling, total love.

"I have to admit, Lucifer, things were always hopping when you were around," God told his former minion.

"Yes, indeed," Lucifer boasted. "You have to admit that I was *the key player* during my time up here!"

Rumor had it that a lot of the creation thing was Lucifer's idea—that's if you believe Lucifer. And in fact, a lot of people did believe Lucifer. People believed because Lucifer gave them what they wanted—a life of doing as they pleased. Like Lucifer, they sought to be gods of their own world even though, also like Lucifer, they did not create their world. The people of Earth had all types of wants and desires. They also had very large egos—and short memories. Lucifer liked it that way.

God summed up Lucifer like this: great idea guy, lousy administrator, extremely ambitious, but has potential. "I would have given him the Universe, but he just needed a little more 'playing time' to get seasoned," God observed. "He was so impatient—ran off with a third of my team—got ahead of his skill set as a leader." With a hint of sadness God concluded, "Oh well, that's what ego does when coupled with free will."

Unaware of God's critique, Lucifer remained wrapped up in himself. "I have no idea how you do anything without me."

"I manage," God demurred. God already knew the answer to the question he was about to ask, but in politeness to his visitor he proceeded. Being polite was good. God was always good. All good, all love—that's God. He asked, "So, Lucifer, what have you been up to?"

"Marketing and promoting," Lucifer relied. He repeated, "Marketing and promoting, marketing and promoting—you know me—always looking ahead."

"New territory?" asked God, again being polite. Remember, he already knew the truth.

"Nope, working the same old territory—Earth. But the difference is that I'm seeking greater penetration. Fools say, 'Less is more.' But, no, no, no! I say *more is more!*"

God liked persistence. Lucifer had a lot of it. Lucifer wouldn't let the Earth go. His goal was one hundred percent domination. With Earth as his base Lucifer would then assault and claim Heaven. God knew all about Lucifer's desires and feared not.

To change the direction of their conversation God made another inquiry. "How's my favorite servant on Earth? Ah...umm...ah..." God paused for effect. "You know..."

"Ha! You forgot!" Lucifer said with glee. "You forgot Job? Gotcha!"

Whenever possible, Lucifer loved to zing God. But you could not really zing God. You could deny his existence, ignore him, or, like Lucifer, fight against him, but you could not zing God.

as possible, which was a lot. He was baiting the hook, so to speak, a big God-sized hook—one not to be ignored.

"Great!" Lucifer exclaimed. Then he caught himself. *The Boss is up to something.* Quickly he said, "Sure, I'm in, but this time we gotta change the rules."

"How?" God was all ears—literally. All ears, all eyes, all…well, you get the picture—infinite variety all the time, all at once. That's God. All love, all knowing, all good—all everything!

"This time, I get to pick the new target," Lucifer offered.

"Suits me. But why?"

"Why? Why?" sputtered Lucifer. "I'll tell you why! Like you don't know that Job was a ringer!"

"A ringer?"

"Yes, a ringer—a setup. The fix was in. I know it."

"Explain…"

(Silence)

Lucifer pouted.

God let him stew for a while. Then dripping with heavenly sweetness, God said, "*Okay—please explain.*" God did not need to ask for anything, but sometimes he bent the rules for Lucifer. It made God feel good. You know—hope for reconciliation, happiness all around, heavenly bliss.

And after being asked so nicely Lucifer could not help but think, *I guess the Boss really still likes me.* "Last time," he told God, "when we started out—Job was the richest guy on all the Earth. We, or more correctly I, upended his life. I took it *all* away. The intent was to get him to dis you and come over to my side. Getting your man—the most blessed one of all—to join in with me would be the beginning of the end for you."

"Lucifer, the thought of taking over from me has become an obsession. It's not healthy, you know."

"I know—I keep failing. It's good for you, unhealthy for me."

God changed the subject, knowing that it did no good to dwell upon it. "I seem to recall a lot of dialogue taking place around Job," He said offhandedly.

"Yeah, Job's wife and friends arrived and they wouldn't shut up." Lucifer looked miffed.

"People do that. They think they are helping."

"Some help! Talk is cheap, you know—real cheap. Me? I don't mince words. I'm a 'do it' kind of guy," Lucifer bragged. He really liked to brag.

"I know—how do I know," confirmed God. Sternly he went on. "Lucifer, you do nothing that gets past me—all of your evil deeds are known. And just because I have not ended your time on Earth does not mean I condone what you do in any way. Do not let my jovial good nature fool you. I am deeply vexed."

As usual, Lucifer ignored what God said. He went on as if his thoughts had not been touched in any way. "Well, what all those useless do-gooders did was talk, and talk, and talk some more…and…and…and…and…"

"…and then?" God helped Lucifer out of his rut with a nudge. God was like that—helpful.

"Thanks!" acknowledged Lucifer. "Back to my point—all that yacking, yacking, yacking—not to mention a wagonload of angst being slathered around. I got sick of all the eternal truths, half-assed ideas, some of your teaching points, and even some of my shtick. It was yadah, yadah, yadah, and it went on forever, or at least it seemed so."

"And your point is…?"

"After all my hard work, and after listening to all their silliness, you just stepped in, wrapped it up with your divine goodness, and made it 'all better' for that miserable schmuck!

"What was wrong with that?"

"After I failed to turn him against you, you made him even richer than before. In fact, you made him filthy rich—*and happy to boot!* Dealing with that is a task for me!"

God enjoyed seeing Lucifer so worked up. *He's so misguided, but I love his tenacious spirit*, God thought. Then he poked at Lucifer by simply saying, "So?"

"So? So! How can I compete with the stuff in the BOOK OF JOB? It shows Job's life as two great peaks of wonderfulness between one long, deep, dark valley of dog doo. You, the Almighty Creator and Bountiful Provider, are associated with your favorite boy being on top of those peaks—first when he is rich, and second, when you made it even better; he's richer. Me! Just look at me. What am I? I'm associated with the middle part—when all the stinky stuff happens. I'm stuck being the valley guy."

"It's better than being a *Valley Girl*!" God laughed heartily at his own joke.

"Ugh." Lucifer sighed at God's humor. "And you wonder why I left?" He sighed longer and heavier than before.

Lucifer never appreciated God's humor; to Lucifer it was lame. Occasionally God would crack a good joke—but it was always squeaky clean. After all, he was God.

Perturbed, Lucifer asked, "Could we continue?"

"As they say, 'you called this meeting.'"

"Yes, I did. Now, to get back on track—this time I pick the target."

"You already said that."

"Do you *always* have to be right?"

"What do you think?"

"Don't do this to me!" exclaimed Lucifer.

"Do what?" God asked. He knew the answer. God knew all the answers. Such was God. It was important for Lucifer to ask the question, and to find the answer—on his own.

"Don't get me off track!" Lucifer said with exasperation.

"How?"

"Asking questions!"

"It is important to find answers. Such is life."

"Do you always have to be so—so—?"

"So…what?"

"Godlike!"

"It's my nature," God confirmed. In a matter of fact, tone, and with solemn dignity he added, "I am the I AM."

"Ugh! I hate that description of you! It's too—too—"

"Too inclusive—too complete? Too all-encompassing—too final?" God could have gone on forever.

"Too everything! It's so over the top. Too...too...too much like God!"

"*But I am God.*"

"That is exactly what I am trying to deal with!" cried Lucifer. "Why do you get to be God?"

There was silence throughout the universe.

God sighed.

After some time, which seemed an eternity, Lucifer asked with forced calmness, "May we return to the original subject?"

"Of course, it's your—"

"Meeting!" completed Lucifer. Frustrated he continued, "Why, why, why do I feel like we've done this before?"

"Before what?" God was having some more fun.

"Stop it, stop it! If we get into one of your time-loop things, I'll quit again!"

"Fine, you can relax—no time loops. *Now, in the present*, let's get back to your ideas on the choice of target."

"Okay, okay. To begin, this time he's not wealthy."

"Interesting...go on."

"Go on? I've got nothing more. We just start with a regular guy— that's it."

"But then what?" God was playing dumb—doing it quite well. As a matter of fact, God did everything quite well. Actually, he did it perfectly. That's God—all love, all good, all everything, all done to perfection.

In response to God's question, Lucifer offered, "We, or more to the point, I, dump on him. Yes, I dump on him Big Time!" Lucifer liked the dumping role. It was easier to tear things down than build them up. *God does his work, I do mine*, Lucifer thought. *He's the yin, and I'm the yang. Or is it the other way around? Whatever.*

"After you dump on him—destroy his life—what then?" asked God.

"Beats me. I just came up with the new start. Let's see how it goes, okay?"

"Deal!" God said.

When God said "deal," it's a bona fide cinch. You could trust God.

Lucifer gave God a thumbs-up, smiled, and said, "Infinite, eternal, all knowing—I have to admit, at times it does make sense for me to trust you."

THE TARGET

God looked down upon the Earth and asked his visitor, "Who did you pick, Luce?"

Lucifer was all smiles because God used his nickname. As an inside joke, God pronounced it as "loose." But joking aside, it was a real honor to have God use your nickname. Especially, if he gave it to you.

Lucifer puffed himself up in recognition of the honor, pointed below at a very ordinary man, and proudly exclaimed, "Him!"

"Who is he?" asked God, feigning not to recognize one of his creations. (Another divine faux pas.)

"Come on, Boss. You know him! That's our guy...he's known officially as Jacob Osborne Brown, Junior!"

"Cute," said God. "His initials are J.O.B. And he is a junior, a second. That makes our guy a Job number two. I like it."

"It's marketing!" crowed Luce. "Like I said, I'm always marketing. Gotta think ahead to identify all the promotional angles."

"Promotional angles?"

"Yes. I'm thinking about the marquee appeal of his name. You know— as presented on billboards and bumper stickers. The eye-appeal image for all the collateral sales items is extremely important. I can see it now on a movie poster. 'The story goes on—you must see Job Two!' or just 'Job 2!' I could use 'Job II!' And maybe even, 'Job, Too!' Is that too far out?

Whatever it is I can see it on tee shirts, coffee mugs, hats—all the usual stuff—and more—much more!"

Lucifer was on a roll. He had always been big into "making a buck."

Lucifer explained where his mind was focused. "For example, right now you and I are about to do a sequel. There are huge spin-off sales opportunities from sequels."

"Really?"

"Now, you *really* are playing dumb."

God winked.

Ignoring the wink Lucifer pressed on, explaining with a question. "Let me ask…how many ROCKY films are there?"

God pretended to think about the answer even though he knew right off. God knew everything. "Including spinoffs?" he pondered aloud to draw the moment out. "Let me see…there's ROCKY…ROCKY II…" He counted on his Godly fingers and finished with, "Six! No! It's seven—and still counting."

"Still counting?" Lucifer asked. "You mean there will be *more*?"

"Appears so…I do like Rocky," God said with a smile.

"Wow! Is Stallone infinite, too?"

Still smiling, God replied, "No. It only seems so."

"Had me fooled. Oh well, it's a good thing I stopped in for a visit anyway. I ought to call my broker and buy more movie stock." (Lucifer was thinking investments for his retirement. You know, the nest egg thing.) "More ROCKY pics—wow! I can't wait!" he happily shouted as he peeked over God's shoulder to observe their target.

****

Jacob Osborne Brown, Junior—Job Number Two—was simply Jake to his friends. Jake lived in a very typical nice house in an average neighborhood. To pay for his ordinary home Jake worked as a middle manager in a non-glamorous, but necessary, business. Jake made toilet paper.

Jake thought he was exceptional, but he was as ordinary as they come.

Jake was certain he was different, and that made him just like everyone else. Thinking he was exceptional while being ordinary actually proved that Jake was not special indeed. It's a paradox. A paradox was one of those "God things."

Jake's wife loved him about as much as other wives of middle managers loved their ordinary middle-manager husbands, which was not very much at all. She secretly wanted an upper-management lifestyle. In her world, lifestyle was everything. There were all types of lifestyles—too many to name. The important thing was to want a better lifestyle. Luce took credit for inventing the lifestyle, as well as lifestyle envy.

Jake's children were typical twenty-first-century kids—meaning they were self-absorbed, spoiled, perpetually bored, and lazy. They did not like or respect their father because they did not know him. They saw no benefit in knowing him. Instead of asking questions or attempting to learn about their father, they wasted most of their precious youth glued to video screens—small ones on phones and larger versions on oversized television sets. When not sitting trance-like before a mega screen they wandered aimlessly through life, staring at handheld ones.

"You know, Luce, not knowing about your father is a common trait," God sadly observed.

"Don't be so touchy, Boss."

"I have a right to be concerned. Once there was nothing, and then I—"

"Yeah, yeah, yeah," interrupted Lucifer. "I've heard this a million times—maybe more."

Tremors permeated the entire Universe.

"Jeez," muttered Lucifer. "Gimme a break. I'm tired of hearing about you being the Creator, and all that goes with it. On Earth we have other interests, you know."

"Other interests—like being tied up in your brand of mischief," God observed as fact, and not a question.

"I don't want to hear your sour grapes over me being out on my own. Besides we have a game going," Lucifer said as he pointed down on Earth. "Just looking at him has me excited. This time I'm gonna win!"

Down below, Jake and most of everyone else were unaware of being watched. Happily ignorant, the people on Earth went about doing their business. Everything was okay. Everyone was in pursuit of a better lifestyle.

Jake was at a place in his life that he described as "more than just okay." Although at times he was vaguely anxious, Jake was very content. Lucifer described him as "fat, dumb, and happy." It was not a paradox. It was his lifestyle. And Jake's lifestyle was about to be turned on its head.

"Hello, Number Two," Lucifer whispered through his most sinister grin. "Get ready. I'm coming to visit you soon."

THE GAME

L ucifer asked, "Boss, will the rules be the same as before?" He was itching to get started and wanted to "do some tearing up and dumping," as he called his activities. "If I remember, I'm limited to just zapping his family and assets, right?"

God felt generous. "Luce, this time you decide. I'll only intervene after he is assaulted by you and reaches out to me. If indeed he does, then it will be my turn. But I'll still allow you to come and go."

"No divine stacked deck this time?" Lucifer asked.

"None, but I must say I am hurt that you would think I broke the rules in any way," he said. God did not break rules. God usually made them. When God made rules they were simple, fair, and just.

Lucifer played his angle. "Then you'll agree that it's okay for my legal department to whip up a few new items for the rule book?"

"It's your show, Luce."

"Deal!"

God knew that when Lucifer said "deal," it meant he would cheat by using the patchwork of incomprehensible rules his lawyers would concoct. God also knew he could step in (as the Creator of All Things), should Lucifer go too far. If needed, God would smooth things out. But that's jumping ahead in this story.

"Here goes!" Lucifer shouted. Eyes red, countenance black, he set to work on an unsuspecting Jake. Hypocritically he sneered, "Hello, my New Best Friend! Look out! I'm back in town and ready to rumble!"

Jake would never consider using the name Luce or call Lucifer a friend, because what was about to happen could never be called friendship. When Lucifer said, "Hey, Friend!" he really meant, "Duck!"

Although Lucifer was very misdirected, God did love his spirit and enthusiasm.

When you had created everything, you would expect others to have a healthy work ethic. God did not like lazy, and Lucifer worked hard at being bad.

With sadness God looked upon Earth and said, "This ought to be interesting. If nothing else, Luce is determined." God then sighed, adding, "I do wish he had stayed with me in Heaven."

THE EVENTS THAT TESTED JAKE

S izing up his totally unaware target, Lucifer mused aloud as he pre-
pared to make his opening move. "Okay, I want him to regret today
more than any day in his puny life. Lucifer squinted and strained. "Let me
see, let me see…hmmmm… It's been a long while since I used one of my
favorites. I think I'll start with an old-fashioned bushwhacking."

Jake was about to be bushwhacked by an expert. Lucifer invented
bushwhacking. He initiated this one with great relish.

There is no warning in a bushwhacking. There is no "Hey, Friend,
look out!" There isn't even a "Duck!"

Here's how the sneak attack played out: down on Jake's part of Earth it
was a normal day, with Jake on his usual way home from the toilet-paper
factory. Traffic was bumper to bumper; the humidity was high—match-
ing the heat at ninety-three. Everyone was testy and irritable. Lucifer
waved his hand and the A/C in Jake's car went kaput. Lucifer loved kaput.

"You are subtle," said God. "Start with small frustrations—the little
things do add up."

"Yep, they sure do. Now, watch this!"

Lucifer added some blaring horns, a mosquito bite, and two pesky
flies (the ones that buzzed incessantly and literally drove you insane).
Although Jake quickly got irritated with his situation he did not act crazy.
He kept his composure.

"Darn," Lucifer said, already bored. "He's Mister Cool and Calm. I need to escalate the tempo of things—get him to react."

God drummed his perfect fingers and watched. *Let's see what he cooks up*, God mused. *He likes to tear down humans because I made them in my image.*

"I want some *real* excitement!" cried Lucifer.

It came in a millisecond, which was simultaneously a long and short time for God.

Lucifer jumped up and down, cheered, and waved his hands. Wham! Jake's car was violently rear-ended and shoved into the one in front of him. Jake experienced multiple injuries, cracked eyeglasses, a broken nose, and a whiplash, just to name a few results from the crash.

Lucifer giggled as he watched a sore and shaken Jake pound on the steering wheel, wince in pain, and scream at the car behind him. "Foul language and road rage will be provided at no extra charge," Lucifer quipped.

The accident tied up traffic and caused frustration and irritation to fester and grow. A lot of people were mad about being delayed. Exchanging insurance information and talking to the police seemed to go on forever. People turned upon each other in an ill-tempered chain reaction, and many of them focused their rage at both Jake and the driver who hit him. Everyone was miserable. Lucifer was beside himself with joy. He danced about giving himself high fives.

Lucifer looked at God, danced some more, and smirked. "Sometimes ya gotta destroy in order to create!"

God nodded, then said, "I know. Remember the flood?"

Lucifer's smirk disappeared. He looked away and muttered, "Always right, always right. Darn, he's always right!" To God he yelled, "I'm not done yet! I've got more!"

God kept to the rules. Although he wanted to, he did not intervene. *I must be patient*, God thought. *I've got time. In fact, I've got all the time there is.*

It was a while before Jake could head for home. Finally he did. And

Jake felt relieved when the nearly demolished family sedan limped into the driveway of his ever so ordinary house. But the relief lasted only for a moment. Soon a new rain of crap began to fall on Jake, compliments of his new bushwhacking friend.

"Duck," whispered Lucifer. "Here come some of my favorite jabs at domestic bliss."

Jake's son Trey sat handcuffed in the rear seat of a police cruiser parked in front of the house. An officer explained that an assault with a deadly weapon incident was more than enough to warrant holding the boy while "some other things were worked out."

"Other things?" a confused Jake asked. "What other things?"

"Dealing, soliciting to deal, conspiring to...well...you know...*things*," answered the policeman.

Jake was speechless.

"Oh! I forgot to mention his jaywalking and littering," the policeman said as he entered the cruiser.

Dumbfounded by the spectacle of his son's arrest, a final message was left ringing in Jake's ears by the policeman: "Oh yeah, and charges for the illegal manufacturing of drugs will be added for the meth lab we found in his bedroom. Also there are some overdue library books still not accounted for. Mister, you've really raised a one-man crime wave."

The lad did not look up as the police car disappeared.

Jake silently stared at his feet, wondering where he had gone wrong with raising his son. "I never saw any of this coming," he mumbled, "never saw it coming, never saw it at all."

Before Jake could reflect or recover, another jab landed. His daughter Elle exited the house and walked past her father without uttering a sound. She headed to the curb, where her pierced and tattooed boyfriend impatiently straddled his idling motorcycle. Elle paused to dab some white powder on her wrist and then snorted it expertly through one nostril.

"C'mon, babe," the boyfriend shouted as he handed her a quart of malt liquor wrapped in a brown paper bag, "we've got places to be and movies to make!" The boyfriend had purchased his bike by directing low-budget porn videos. Elle, his current star, gulped from the offered bottle, washed down a double dose of Molly, and mounted behind him on the cycle. Boyfriend revved the cycle and they disappeared.

Jake stood before his home in total shock as a million thoughts ping-ponged inside his head. Even though his children had routinely ignored him, Jake loved them deeply. Tears ran down his cheeks.

"Got 'em good!" Lucifer bragged as he danced his little shuffle step again.

"I'd say so," God commented flatly. "Think he's had enough?"

"Nope," answered Lucifer. "I've got more. Watch this!"

Just then, Mrs. Brown—Jennifer—known as Jen-Jen to her most intimate friends, exited the house in the company of Lionel, a male neighbor. They were leaving to set up a new household—in honor of Lionel's promotion into the ranks of upper management. He worked for the local grocery store, where the two met daily to engage in trysts, taking place in a stockroom under the watchful eye of the store's security camera. Unknown to Lionel and Jen-Jen, the store's staff scheduled their breaks around the couple's dalliances, which they recorded and watched more religiously than the most popular soap opera. Also unknown to the pair was that a triple X collection of the couple's most heated moments was about to be launched on YouTube, Netflix, HBO, and HULU. Elle's boyfriend had arranged the editing, packaging, and promotion.

"Jennifer!" cried Jake in dismay. "Where are you going?"

"Away!" she replied. "I am getting away from you, you pitiful loser. I am leaving to be with someone who can give me the things I want." She pointed at Lionel's car. "That is a 7 series BMW!"

The car was crammed full with her suitcases and clothing bags.

"Com'on, Jen-Jen," Lionel coaxed. "We're running late for my promotion party." He flashed a toothy grin and quickly guided her toward the car. They were gone in an instant. The BMW was as fast as it was expensive.

"Quite a show," God said with a twinge of remorse in his voice. "Are you finished?"

"Oh, no! Now, for frosting the cake!" squealed Lucifer.

In a daze Jake walked zombie-like toward his home's front door. On the way, he trod through three (count 'em three!) piles of dog poop. Lucifer loved dog poop. Lucifer took credit for inventing it. God never challenged his claim.

God observed Lucifer's handiwork. "Very effective final insult—he indeed is ruined."

Lucifer beamed.

"Why the change in tactics?" God inquired. "Last time you killed his children straightaway."

"I'm flattered," replied Lucifer, glad that God noticed. But then again God didn't miss much. In fact, he didn't miss anything. "I admit this not my usual style, but it is more effective in the long run."

"It is a new approach for you," God said.

"It'll work, trust me," asserted Lucifer. "I've learned—oh, how I have learned!"

"Care to share?" God liked to rhyme. God also liked silly songs, warm out-of-the-oven banana bread, and thin-crust pizza. He was not fond of lint, selfishness, bad breath, and of course, dog poop.

"It's simple," Lucifer explained. "If people are dead they cannot continue to hurt one another."

"True."

"Yep. Just look at what people have done to him."

God looked down at Jake and saw a thoroughly defeated human being. God frowned and then sighed. The light level of the universe briefly dimmed.

Lucifer grinned widely. "For humans, their satisfaction and meaning are tied up in material things. They think they think, but they do not think at all—they only want. In the old days it was just material things that I took away. But now I've added a new dimension—misery caused by those he loved. Look at him—the pain will go on and on and on. He will have to contend with lawyers, alimony, child support, bail, jail, and rehab. Last time, I killed off Job's family and took away his wealth and health. But then you simply replaced everything. Not this time. Now this guy has the steady drip, drip, drip of all that hurt emanating from others."

"Indeed, Luce, you are a wonder!"

Coming from God any compliment meant a lot. Lucifer enjoyed being good at being bad. To God he boasted, "I think I'll copyright my motto!"

The Conversations

#1

On Earth, where Lucifer had been targeting all his attentions, information was quickly shared between its inhabitants. News, or what passed for it, moved on airwaves, satellites, wires, and word of mouth, just to name some of the methods. Yet prayer—talking or communicating with God—was passé. It was seldom used. Moreover, it was barely mentioned. At least that was the perception by God. And he should know.

God listened to prayers, and prayer volume had been steadily decreasing on earth. Jake did not pray. That was okay with God—he still cared. God never stopped listening, and caring, even if people did not pray very much.

When people who knew Jake heard about his misfortunes, some were oddly glad. Germans call that feeling *Schadenfreude*—the joy one experiences over learning about the misfortune of others. The Germans named it, but Lucifer invented *Schadenfreude*.

Since leaving God's team Lucifer filled the Earth with many additional things that made life irksome. Irksomeness was a Lucifer thing. So was vexation.

Other Lucifer inventions: lawyers, mosquitoes, late fees, burnt toast, nonfat dry milk, and diarrhea. He also chaired the meeting that produced the designated hitter rule in baseball. To be fair, Lucifer abstained during the vote because he had played shortstop on the best team in Heaven during his stint there as God's Number Two. He also invented boils, bad breath, acne, hot flashes, and toe jam. Lucifer always got the chuckles when he thought about toe jam.

"So, Luce," asked God, "what's next?"

"Sure, *like you don't know.*" Lucifer pointed at Jake's house. "Before, with the first Job, we let life play out for a while. Now, I'm—"

"Works for me," God interrupted.

"No, no, no! Not this time! Like I said, this time will be different. I'll own him—just watch. His friends will come and go. And then be gone forever. They'll offer advice and opinions, all of which will confuse and muddle his thinking. You stay out of this. In the end he will believe that you let it all happen. At that point I'll be his anchor—then I'll win!"

"I take it that you sent divorce papers...and a pink slip?"

"Yep, the pink slip was easy. His job was kaput as soon as the videos of his wife and daughter hit the Internet." Lucifer giggled and said, "Get this—the HR department at the toilet-paper factory was told to 'clean up the crap in his life!'" Lucifer doubled over in laughter. "They found a way to fire him—like they always do—and they made it funny to boot!"

"What about his wife?"

"Deeply embarrassed and emotionally injured by the videos, but able to soak him in the divorce, nonetheless."

"Really?"

"Yep, she blamed him for her sexual excesses. Claimed she was 'forced' into promiscuity because he worked so much and neglected 'her needs.' The judge was sympathetic. He liked watching her in the videos."

"That doesn't seem fair."

"Nothing says it has to be fair. It's all about winning."

Lucifer had set up the legal system. Remember, he invented lawyers.

****

Sometime later, actually on the day after his divorce was final, Jake put on a world-class garage sale. The idea came from his pals—the people he could trust most—the guys and one gal who were members of his fast-pitch softball team, the Misguided Saints.

Over many years, through thick and thin, the Saints were Jake's best and most loyal friends. They never missed a chance to "be there" for Jake. In this case it meant conducting a garage sale to get rid of all the stuff associated with Jake's past life. It was also the perfect excuse to toss some meat on the barbeque grill, chug down some brews, and give their friend advice on how to "get beyond the pain," "kick start your next phase of life," "go to the next level," and… Well, you get the picture.

"I love these guys," said Lucifer. "They focus on my kind of stuff—half-baked ideas born out of copious alcohol consumption."

Seriously—on Earth alcohol and bad advice go together.

The first of Jake's friends to arrive was Larry, his closest pal from all the way before high school. Although he had entered community college on a GED and quickly flunked out, Larry thought he knew everything. He did not. God knew everything. Larry thought he was God. Larry was wrong. Even Lucifer did not think *he* was God. Lucifer had aspirations, but he was not crazy. Larry was crazy.

Lucifer 1, Larry 0.

Larry plopped into a lawn chair with a beer. It was 7 a.m. Larry could drink beer at any time. "I see you've experienced a *little* trouble in the flow of life," Larry said following a belch. Larry belched a lot. He could also underestimate things. "I'd say, your life was real good, until it wasn't."

"You could say that," answered Jake.

"I just did."

It was an awkward moment.

Larry asked, "So…what's your plan?"

"I'm moving forward. Gonna focus on improving my life through relaxation, a high-fiber diet, and yoga." All things considered, Jake was even-keeled, relaxed, and calm.

"You seem very relaxed." Larry also liked to state the obvious.

"Well, my life as I've known it is pretty much over. Wife—gone. Kids—in trouble *and gone*. My job is gone, too. I'm in debt, nearly broke, and I have a whopper of a cold that hangs on and on. But all things considered, I am okay. But what really bugs me is all the dog poop in my yard."

Lucifer knew that at times it truly was the little things that could drive people absolutely nuts and push them over the edge. He was hoping to break Jake's calmness by assaulting him with countless small jabs. "Death by a thousand tiny paper cuts," was how Lucifer described his approach.

Larry jumped in. (Not the dog poop.) Instead, the topic of conversation was Jake's woes. "The dog poop is a symbol," Larry asserted. "It represents something—maybe something very significant."

"I think it just represents dog poop," Jake told him.

"No, it's karma. I'm certain of it." Larry was playing God again—in his own mind. "Karma is what I'd call it."

"Call it what you like, but it stinks!" Jake exclaimed with frustration at both Larry and the smell coming from his shoes.

"I don't think you understand," said Larry (speaking again as God). "Trust me, it's karma! Don't you believe in karma?"

"No, I do not."

"Well, even if you don't, you should. It's real and it affects you—everyone knows that!"

"So if you believe in the bogeyman, and I don't, then I should still be afraid?"

"I don't follow," Larry said with more honesty about his cluelessness than he knew.

"I know you don't follow. You miss a lot."

"Like what?" Larry said as half challenge and half question.

Jake pointed to Larry's shoes. "You've stepped in dog poop, pal."

"Oh crap!"

"Yep, now you've got it."

"Got what?"

"Karma—the brown smelly kind."

"Funny—real funny," muttered Larry as he stepped out of the garage to clean the smelly mess off his shoes.

****

Up above, God could not help but comment, "Luce, that's a long way to go just for a poop joke."

"I know, I know, but I've got this thing about it. I only wish I had invented dog poop."

"You did."

"Really? I thought you did."

"Not a chance."

"You missed a ton of opportunities for some really hilarious gags with the stuff."

"Let's move on," suggested God. Peering down on Earth, he asked, "So what's next?"

"As if you didn't know..."

(Pause)

God did not take the bait.

"Okay, it's time for what I call 'the community parade of idiots' to get rolling. I'm arranging for an assortment of Jake's well-wishing friends and nosey neighbors to drop in to dispense misguided wisdom."

"Let me guess—the ultimate source of their wisdom would be *you*?"

"Bingo!"

Lucifer loved to shout, "Bingo!" (More about that later.)

*****

A visitor appeared in Jake's garage door. It was Beth, from across the street. She addressed Jake with, "Hello, Jacob." Beth did not know or care that friends called him Jake. Beth was not a friend. She was a nosey neighbor. But she could be a friend. This was Beth's opportunity.

"I couldn't help but notice all the commotion," Beth said as she eyed the items assembled for the garage sale. "Did you know there is a strange man in your yard swearing up a storm over something on his shoes?"

"Thank you for your concern, Beth," Jake responded. "It's thoughtful of you to warn me." Jake was being nice. It's nice to be nice. Jake needed a new friend, one who did not say, "Duck!" or get uppity when it was pointed out that one's feet were covered in poop.

Beth did not see that Jake's reply was an invitation for a friendly exchange. Instead, Beth feigned interest in an item or two while she moved about the garage in a listless manner. Finally, she lit upon an old TV set. After turning it on and racing through some stations, she addressed Jake again. "Jacob, this TV is broken. Did you know that whatever channel you set it on it only plays two? It's either the Home Shopping Network or an Indian evangelist shouting about sending him *seed money*, which is odd because there's no way he's a farmer.'"

"Yeah, it's my answer for Alzheimer's," joked Jake. "The show's content is always new."

"It's not funny to make jokes about Alzheimer's," Beth said sharply.

"I meant no harm," Jake explained. "In my situation, my life needs some levity. If I cannot make jokes, what do I have?"

Beth assumed a serious demeanor. To Jake she inexplicably grew in size. Beth looked that way when she was about to nose into someone's business. Through a stare called the "Stink Eye," she said, "It may be none of my business, but—"

****

Oh, so correct, thought God. He did not like nosey neighbors.

Go for it, girl! urged Lucifer. Nosey neighbors were one of his favorite tools.

****

Stink Eye Beth continued. "—the person to blame for the change in your life is no real surprise to me." She gave him a mega stink eye. Her tone was accusatory and definitely not friendly. Beth was missing her chance to be a friend by the widest margin possible.

Jake was incredulous at her statement. "You mean all my troubles are no surprise to you? Like in *I am responsible*? You can't be serious."

"Yes, I am! It is your fault," asserted Beth. She moved toward Jake like a snake toward a mouse. "I've watched what happened around here. You never were at home. You were always gone, and—"

Jake interrupted her assault. "Always gone? That's an impossibility."

Beth paused to think. "Well, yes...theoretically... But I meant *almost always*. It's very plain to see that if you had been a better provider and been here more, your wife would not have run off."

"So let me get this straight. You are saying that if I were wealthier and at home more, it would have made my wife a more moral person?"

"Well...well...yes. It's so obvious. Your wife cheated on you and left because you neglected her," Beth said with a smug, self-righteous look. "That man she left with is now giving her more of what she needs and wants."

Initially Jake was deflated. He thought Beth's visit was meant to be a positive experience. Instead, she had come to play a game of I TOLD YOU SO!

People love to say, "I told you so!" Luce taught them how.

They also like to say, "If it were up to me, I would _____ (you fill in)."

And, "I think you should _____ (you fill in)."

A very popular one is, "Everyone believes _____ (you fill in)."

****

Good! Lucifer thought. *If you give them half a chance, people will tell you how to live your life even when they are so misled themselves. Her meddling advice would even be better mixed with alcohol.*

****

Jake thought for a while, then said, "Beth, imagine the following scenario. If *your* husband is gone away from home, then it is okay that *you'll cheat on him with some guy that has more money, right?*"

Beth was shocked by the thought. "What on earth are you saying?"

Jake continued giving her some of what she had given him. "I'm saying—no, asking—when do you plan to fool around?"

"No—I'm not—no! That's wrong!"

"But it's your logic."

"I…I…I…"

"…will do it." He finished the thought for her. "Yes, you will! If you just follow your own logic, you'll do exactly the same as my wife. You will fool around."

With as much indignation as she could muster, Beth shouted, "Jacob Brown, you evil man! You are sick! You are a perverted sick man! No wonder your wife left you! And I am leaving, too!" She stormed across the street back to the safety of her nosey-neighbor perch.

Watching her speed away, Jake sighed. "I don't feel any better for doing that. She thinks that marriage is just about money and status. I did not enjoy telling her what a fool she is, but it needed to be done."

****

"She's not far off base," Lucifer said. "Money is a big part of the mix, but there are other elements in play, too. Sometimes it's not at all about the money, the prizes, or who amasses the most toys. Sometimes it is just about shouting, 'Bingo!'" Lucifer liked to win, and when he did, he especially liked shouting, "Bingo!"

****

CLAP! CLAP! CLAP! The applause came from Larry. "That went well!" he said. His feet were clean, but his thoughts were not. He liked being the bearer of bad news. "Maybe she was right. Maybe you deserve all of the bad stuff that has landed on you. Canned from your job, divorced, one kid in jail, and the other one a wannabe porn star. Hasn't it crossed your mind that maybe God did this to you for a reason? Maybe a good one at that."

Jake deflated immediately. Despair showed on his face like a death mask. He slumped into a lawn chair and asked, "Larry, do you think there's a cosmic scale of justice?"

"You mean like your good and bad deeds being weighed against each other?" Larry asked and then answered himself. "Of course I do. In the East it's karma—here it's God's justice come home."

Jake attempted a weak joke. "Could it possibly be part of my permanent record?"

Larry ignored his friend's attempt at humor. He had some bogus wisdom to impart. "If there is a cosmic scale, you may have indeed tipped it. Maybe you built up a pile of wrongs so offensive that God had to take action. I'd say it's payback time in God's accounting system."

*****

Up above, God asked, "Do they really think I'd do that?"

It was a rhetorical question. A rhetorical question is one that really needs no answer. All questions were rhetorical ones for God.

*****

Jake mused aloud, "Payback could be an explanation. But I'm not buying it. That would make God as petty as us."

*****

Again up above, God liked what he heard. God exclaimed, "Good boy!" Joy rolled across the cosmos.

"Quiet!" Lucifer hissed. "You'll influence the results, and that's not fair. You said you'd not intervene like that. The rules are that I do the active stuff and you cannot appear to the target unless and until he clearly convinces me that he's in your camp and not mine."

"Okay," God said. "I'll stick to just listening." God again was polite, not mentioning Lucifer's contradictory position about fairness. God said, "I may not appear to be actively influencing every instance of life, but I do keep track. After all, it is my Universe."

"Whatever!"

Lucifer was peeved. Getting peeved at God was natural for him. That's why he had split away from God and left Heaven. Lucifer wanted to run the Universe. He really wanted to be God. The trouble for Lucifer was that, although he was an expert at manipulating all things in the Universe, being adept at combining parts of the Universe into new configurations and even creating on a small scale he could not do what God had done. God spoke the Universe into existence. Lucifer envied what God had done and he could not do. Envy fed his ego and drove Lucifer into darkness—the place where there was no God.

****

On Earth Jake mused some more. "If God was that way—you know, petty—well, would he really be God?"

"It's something to think about. Maybe it's true," Larry offered. "Or maybe you screwed up and God is just getting even. Or even worse, you screwed up really bad and he's going easy on you now, preparing to drop a bigger hammer later—maybe he will strike you dead."

"No, no, that can't be it," Jake said with determination. "I don't think God did any of this to me. If God had the power to create something as big as the Universe, I doubt that he would waste his time on causing my tiny set of troubles. He's bigger than that."

"Don't be so quick to dismiss the idea," Larry countered. "*Everyone believes* that God is the source of evil as well as good. Don't fight it with your limited skills of reason. Just go with it as a belief—a widely held belief."

Does the "everyone believes it" line sound familiar?

It did to Jake.

He responded forcefully. "I don't care what everyone believes. My ability to reason tells me that any payback, karma, or mystical forces involved in my woes are not from God. When reason sleeps all kinds of monsters appear, and my power to reason is all I have to hold back when the monsters attack me. It stands to reason that a creator would not destroy his own creation. In my heart, I don't want to imagine it any other way. And at times I feel as if the Devil himself is dragging me away from whatever is really good in my life."

"Dude, you're not that important."

"Well, sometimes I think I am!"

"How can *you* be so sure?"

"I don't know how I'm sure. I just am.

****

Up above, God smiled and the light in all of God's creation amped up a notch.

Lucifer shouted, "Crap!" Hardly anyone heard him.

#2

A voice came from a figure quietly listening in the corner. "Jake, when I look at what happened to you, all I can see is yellow flashing lights." It was Kyle, the team's longtime bench warmer. "If it was up to me I'd play it safe, be cautious, lay low, hide my name tag. Your mantra should be easy does it...easy does it...easy does—"

"It figures, you wimp!" interrupted Larry. "Kyle, you never saw a challenge you wouldn't avoid." He grabbed Kyle's hat, tossed it aside, placed him in a headlock, and began administering a vigorous noogie.

"Ow!" Kyle cried out. "Stop! That hurts! Stop!"

Larry rubbed harder and faster. "I'll stop the noogies when you quit telling Jake to lay low. He's broke and needs a job! Uncle? Uncle? Say, 'Uncle!'"

"Okay! Okay!" Kyle blurted. "I give in—Uncle!"

Larry released him. "Now is not the time for Jake to be cautious. He needs to 'go for it,' 'tempt the fates,' 'push the edge of the envelope.'"

"Sure—sure—sure," chanted Kyle. "But listen to me—listen! I heard what he said about God. And I disagree."

"Tell me your side of things," Jake said.

"It's simple. All that belief stuff is important but, Jake, you must shape and tone your actions in light of what other people think about life and God. You have to and must blend in."

"Okay, I get it," Larry said, nodding toward Jake. "You're saying Jake should go with the flow one hundred percent."

"Right!" agreed Kyle. "Go with the flow!"

****

Up above, God said, "I don't like the sound of 'go with the flow.'"

"I do," grinned Lucifer. "If Jake follows his friend's advice, I've got him. I'll win! Here, Boss, look at this." He pulled out a folder, took out a couple of pages, and waved them before God. Lucifer was referring to a recent study indicating that on Earth he was doing quite well versus God. Lucifer invented the phrase "according to a recent study of (fill in with whatever you want)" as a means to convince people to do all sorts of foolish things.

The study's title revealed why Lucifer was so excited. "People Grow Skeptical of God" was in big bold letters. The study revealed that in the past three decades the number of people who believe in God had decreased by half, and the number praying had declined fivefold.

"It appears that people have lost faith in you," Lucifer said with unbridled pride. "And it won't be long before the target of our contest agrees with them, too!"

God frowned. God was sad. His sadness was for the people who did not pray. God enjoyed listening to prayers and he enjoyed answering them, too.

On Earth Lucifer appeared to be winning. He very badly wanted Jake to be in his fold. "Go with the flow, Jake," Lucifer whispered. "Go with the flow."

****

"But what if I really do believe in something and it's unpopular?" Jake queried his friends. "Do I just lie about what I believe?"

"Sure, particularly if you're doing it to get along. You know, to please people. You don't want to offend anyone," Kyle replied. "Your goal in life should be to fit in."

"I agree," Larry chimed in without noticing the irony of his statement in light of his recent remarks. Previously he told Jake to stretch the envelope, and now he wanted Jake to hide inside it.

"I don't know," Jake countered. "I'm not convinced that being agreeable just to be agreeable will improve my lot in any way. I want to live by my convictions—my beliefs."

****

"Those idiots!" shouted Lucifer. "We almost had him. Their motto should be 'We're slow, but we do poor work.' I can't stand it when a trend reverses—even a little bit. It particularly irks me when dopes like Larry and that other fool are not getting the job done. Looks as if I'll have to go down there to pitch a few balls myself. The best place to toss a lie is between two truths, and if those fools can't influence Jake any better, I guess that I'm going to aim my best stuff right between the tidbits of truth that Jake relies upon."

"And what might your best stuff be," asked God, "sliders, or curves?"

Lucifer, forgetting that God invented the baseball analogy, tried another route. He boasted, "No! I'll use a new approach—one that really works—my latest version of the seven deadly sins: greed, sex, violence, virtual violence, preoccupation with trivia, political correctness, and celebrity worship."

"That's quite a list."

"You bet it is! I've got most of the world in a state of chaos with what I've done. There is no culture, or even a counterculture, anymore. People are chasing about filled with half-baked ideas that I constantly toss their way. Right now I've got them actually following imaginary sports."

"You are referring to fantasy football?"

"Yep! Even the real stuff isn't good enough," bragged Lucifer.

"That is absolutely amazing! So what is your goal?"

"You gotta be kidding! It's the same old, same old thing. One day I'm gonna run *everything*!"

"Luce, along with your persistence, I am amazed by your ambition."

"Well, you ought to be, 'cause one day I am going to win and you'll be in the unemployment line. For instance, now—right now on Earth—I've got a good number of them not believing in you and the rest believe that I do not exist. You get it? I can win both ways!"

"How does that work?"

"They've lost faith in you and I'm not a threat. So as soon as I get them to accept my temptations as their normal desires, I will have total control over them. And when I have all of Earth doing my bidding, it will be mine forever. You'll be cut out of your own creation and I'll have a permanent safe base—not one you merely allow me to play with."

#3

"Jake, maybe it would help if you went to church." The advice came from Keith, the consummate team player.

"What will I find at church?" Jake asked.

"A lot of smart people. Nice ones, too," Keith told him.

Larry, always up for a tussle, snidely tossed his view into the mix. "At church I've found that there are only three kinds of people—those who count and those who don't."

Confused, Keith uttered, "Huh? What you said doesn't add up. That's only two kinds of people."

"Okay," blurted Larry, "I'll amend my list—there are smart ones, good looking ones, and rich ones—that's three—and it's the three kinds of people you see at *my* church."

"At *my* church, Unity Village, we focus on sharing the positive experience of praise and worship," Keith quickly countered. "In the past, attending church was all about enduring stale liturgy and boring sermons. Now, at Unity, we joyously sing, share joy with one another, and hear a relevant message, which is always inspirational. After that we sing some more before breaking for refreshments, which usually include some wonderful homemade baked goods made with healthy ingredients."

"Healthy baked goods!" blurted Larry. "What's next, low-cal donuts—with bigger holes? Jake, you must come to the Universal Cathedral of Goodness. It has the message on how you can be a winner again. Get this, our leader Pastor Donny Joel is so successful. He and his wife, the beautiful Chrissie, receive no salary from the congregation. Instead, they live the life of success based solely on the book and video sales of their messages delivered at the cathedral. I've been to Keith's place and all I can say is 'no thanks' to a message supported by free cookies. I don't want what he's got."

"What is it about the message at Unity you don't like?" Jake asked.

"It's loser worship. The Kumbaya happy type, where miserable people with poor habits waste their time and yours with useless routines and rituals."

"I beg your pardon," replied an indignant Keith. "Our practices—what you call useless rituals—are important!"

"Beg pardon back," Larry wheezed as he inhaled some beer. "Your meetings are full of mere controlling routines played over and over and over by weak losers wanting to dominate even weaker ones. Jake, you need to get over the negative happenings in your life by being with winners—real winners." Larry kept drinking, then added, "I think, maybe God isn't mad at you after all—maybe you just haven't heard the right message."

"What is the right message?" Jake demanded.

"The message," shouted Larry, "is that God loves winners!"

"I thought he loved everyone," Keith countered with a huff.

"Yeah, yeah—I've heard that, but it's only half the message," asserted Larry as he chewed on a hunk of breakfast burrito and quickly washed it down with more beer. "It's so simple—everyone loves a winner, especially God."

"What about the less fortunate?" Jake asked.

"He loves them, too—just not as much." Larry was on a roll. "It makes sense. The winners get the best treatment in life—you know, health, wealth, public acclaim. The losers, if they are lucky, get to ride along, participating in the process. You know, they do the feel-good churchy stuff while they benefit from the efforts of the winners." He looked to Keith for affirmation.

Keith went blank, then whispered, "I dunno. I dunno."

"See!" Larry exclaimed. "Keith's 'I dunno' proves my point. Just pass through the parking lots of both our churches—that'll convince you. High-end rides versus minivans and cheap SUVs."

"Like, maybe at the cathedral I'll see a familiar Series 7 BMW?" Jake asked.

"Yeah, yeah—sure!" answered the not-so-smart Larry.

"No, thanks. I'll pass." Jake rolled his eyes and continued. "I think people deserve nothing from God. It's that simple. Everything we have is a gift from our creator. We have been given life and are owed nothing and deserve nothing."

"Pastor Donny would disagree," said Larry.

"I'd expect nothing else," Jake replied. "I'm certain his message is that God means only to drape us in riches—with the biggest share going to the winners."

"Yes!" cried Larry. "Like I said, God loves winners!"

Jake shook his head. "It's déjà moo."

"Huh?" uttered Larry.

Jake answered, "I've heard that bull before." Everyone burst into laughter, except Larry. His face assumed a concrete pout. Jake said to him, "God made billions of losers—and I'm one of them. I've suffered great losses and I hurt—a lot. I'm certainly not a winner by any of Pastor Donny's standards, and I certainly don't want to be like the butthole my wife went for. Pastor Donny has nothing for me. The prosperity message he is known for doesn't work when hard times hit. Suffering is real and inescapable. And it's valuable in its own right. It's what tests our mettle."

"So you'll come to my church, the Unity Village?" Keith asked.

"I think not," answered Jake.

"Why?" Keith demanded uncharacteristically.

"Because everyone has different flaws, which are distributed and exposed for each of us in a variety of ways."

"I don't follow," Keith said.

"A one-size-fits-all remedy for billions of people doesn't make sense for me. Rituals, routines, and chanted prayers are not the way to go, in my humble opinion," explained Jake. "I think each person is on their own journey and the path for each is individual and unique. I'll find things in my own way.

****

"I don't like the way this is going," muttered Lucifer. "This guy is proving to be a poor choice. He's not the small-time putz and shallow thinker I took him for."

"Remember, he was your choice," God said, snickering ever so slightly.

"Stop it!" yelled Lucifer. "Stop with that 'choice' mantra you like so much. Pretty soon you'll be doing one of your mind-game, time-loop thingies again, using it to explain everything."

"You mean like, infinite choices must lead eventually to the one possibility of returning a perfect universe where unity, the singularity, returns and—?"

"STOP IT! I SAID STOP!"

"Okay, but it was your—?"

"Choice! Choice! Choice! CHOICE!" he yelled. "Are you happy now?"

"Perhaps this was not such a good idea. Maybe we should just call it quits. I'll even let you have a draw," offered God.

"No, don't go there!" Lucifer responded quickly. "I asked for it and I'm going to see it through. Last time, I just eased out of the picture and Job remained in your camp without an extended effort by me. I'm going on. No, more than that—I aim to prevail. I'll get him to deny you and join with me. Like other humans, he'll start by making little deals—for money and pleasures of the flesh. In the end he'll deal away his soul. Others have done it. All I need is some time."

#4

Meanwhile, back on Earth…

"Can't we all just get along?" asked Jason, the team's utility infielder and all-around good guy. "As things go we really are decent people, but there can be so much more division within a group of nice guys like us than in a gang of professional criminals."

"Look! Mister Good Guy has finally decided to speak!" taunted a renewed Larry. "Please, grace us with your wisdom!"

Jason, nodded, smiled, and got up from his folding chair. He was used to Larry. "It is simply a matter of misguided preoccupation," he matter-of-factly explained.

"Ha!" Larry blurted. "With you everything is simple." And before Jake could interject, or Keith could utter, "I dunno," Larry added loudly, "Explain!"

Unflustered, Jason shared his thought. "Although the bad guys agree to focus on evil acts, you chaps are too self-absorbed to agree on anything."

"That's it?" Larry questioned. "That's all you've got?"

"Yes, that's it."

There was a long silent pause—a standoff between teammates. Larry bent first, and in defeat he waved for Jason to proceed. "The floor is yours."

"I heard you talk about churches—about which one is better, yours or Keith's. Actually, both are deficient. They only exist so that the people who want to attend get something. And what they get does not matter. Ancient scriptures, from all the world's cultures, speak of self-control, self-denial—certainly not how much stuff you can collect, how good you can feel, and certainly not self-worship. Most churches today are peddling self-esteem, self-love, self-assertion, and even self-forgiveness. God is rarely mentioned; it's all 'me, me! Me!' If and when God is described, it's only as some sort of ATM in the sky pumping out health, wealth, and giddy self-absorbed feelings."

"If we are so wrong, what is right?" asked Larry. "Inform us mortals. What do *you* believe?"

"It is not what I believe that is important," Jason shared. "It is what I question."

Everyone stared at him as if he had found gold.

He continued. "Doubt is where we must begin the process of believing, and you can't even start if you spend all your time worrying and scheming to get more than the next guy. That way makes it everyone against everyone. Look, me versus you and us versus them are not really the best ways to run the world. Rather, it should be everything versus the Truth."

"Yeah, but what *is* the Truth?" asked Larry. "And don't gimme your own version of a Keithism. Not another 'I dunno.' Tell us what the Truth is!"

Jason got very serious. "Truth just is. It has no agenda. It needs no defense—at least by defenders like us. Truth defends itself just by being. And Truth is pure—it's like a piece of divinity." Pleased with his definition, Jason sat down, nodded, and crossed his arms as if he'd delivered a final ultimatum to a foe.

"Pie-in-the-sky simplistic BS," chided Larry. Unaffected by Jason's speech, he said, "I prefer one of Keith's 'I dunnos' over your hunk of 'Truth is just itself' smoke-and-mirror vagueness."

"Larry, you indeed are a cynic," Jake replied.

"Cynic, no. World-class realist, yes!"

"Okay, I can't argue with your nature, beer soaked as it is," Jake said. "But what's your point?"

Larry stood up as if to preach like Donny Joel. He was all SMILE. "I go with what I know. Just look at the news and consider this: what happens when the Truth, to be true, has to be impartial? It will tell us bad news! If Truth is true, then it has to tell us about how the strong and clever dominate and abuse the weak-minded. It has to tell the good and the bad. Just this morning, in the same day's news, terrorists duped a group of slow-witted women into becoming suicide bombers, and here, where we are so much more advanced, a sicko police detective, one of our 'finest in blue,' with the aid of his girlfriend, forced a thirteen-year-old runaway girl into prostitution. Evil is evil and it is everywhere, and Truth represents equally all the crap in this world along with the good stuff. Good news, bad news—that's the only Truth I know."

"I don't know much," Keith admitted, "but that's a hard line of reasoning to refute."

Now it was Jake's turn to criticize Keith's "I dunno" routine. He turned on him, asking, "For Pete's sake, Keith, what *do* you know?"

Keith scrunched his brow. Being put on the spot made him very uncomfortable, and he sat silent, unmoving for what seemed like forever. Just as Larry was about to give him a snap-out-of-it noogie, Keith spoke. He began clearly and slowly. "What I know is that I'm scared a lot of the time. Even though we live in a great place, far from war, richer that most of the world, with ample food, and comfortable safe homes, I'm still scared. When you are in a miracle, you cannot see it and definitely you cannot appreciate it. But nightmares are very different. When you are in them all you want is to get out. Stories like the ones Larry shared convince me that I'm in a nightmare, not a miracle. Did you know that we have a gun that can shoot a million rounds per minute? It is aptly named the METAL STORM. Who builds and uses that kind of weapon—dreamers of miracles? I don't think so. Kind souls don't think up things like that. Nightmare creatures are behind 'em. Evil is in control, or at the very least it is quite good at getting us to do what it wants." Keith sat upon a stack of old magazines and softly added, "Maybe my saying 'I don't know' is just a short prayer based upon exasperation, or maybe it's an 'I don't know what to do.' Maybe it's a prayer simply asking for help from above. I don't want to rely upon people—especially after what I know about Kitty Genovese."

"This I gotta hear," Larry sniped. "She must be one of the many women that dumped you."

Keith stared at Larry and said, "Not funny. This is real. It happened in March 1964. She was attacked on a street in New York City. When she screamed for help people heard her, but they did nothing. The attack went on. She yelled, pleaded, and begged for someone help—to stop the attacker. No one helped and she was murdered in their midst, only a few steps from her home. I just cannot trust people knowing what happened to Kitty Genovese. Life scares me."

(Silence)

Finally, the silence ended. Larry apologized. He said softly, "I didn't mean to bum you out, man."

"Yeah, me, too," added Jason, just as softly.

"Yeah, I'm sorry," whispered Jake.

#5

"You boys look like Mommy put you all in time-out," joked Brienne as she rearranged some of the items on the front table of the yard sale. "It's either that or you ran out of beer," she added with a smile.

Brienne was the team's pitcher, and its only female member. Well known for her quick mind and equally quick fastball, Brienne had negotiated her way through college on a joint athletic-academic scholarship to become a top-rated forensic accountant. No hidden number, obscure thought, theory, or riddle could get past her agile mind, plus she could more than hold her own as the sole non-male Misguided Saint. Her presence always raised her teammate's spirits, Jake's in particular.

"Traffic for the yard sale has been slow," explained Jake, bringing her up to speed. "We've been solving the world's problems along with all its associated theological issues—just to kill time. Trouble is that we're better at killing the friendly mood."

"Beats cannibalism," quipped Brienne.

Deer-in-the-headlights Keith uttered his incomprehension with another "I don't understand." Jake and Jason nodded their agreement, Larry opened another beer, and with motherly concern and great skill, Brienne successfully fended off his poorly aimed slap at the back of Keith's head, grabbing Larry's hand and forcefully bending his fingers backward.

A loud "Ow!" erupted from Larry.

Brienne held on and casually offered an explanation of her point without missing a beat. "As terrible as humans can be to one another in advancing their own positions, the only taboo is that we do not routinely eat each other. That would put an end to all the fun activities such as slavery, torture, and maiming, which I may want to get into with you, Larry, if you cannot stop picking on Kyle and Keith." She applied more pressure.

"Okay—okay! Just let go!" pleaded Larry.

"Promise, no more head slaps—no more noogies. Understand?"

"Yes! Yes!" Larry exclaimed. "Just let me go!"

"Say it's a deal."

"Deal—it's a deal!" blurted Larry.

Brienne glared at him and then let go. She looked at Jake and said, "This is your party—tell me everything that's been going on."

Jake quickly recapped the morning's conversations in every detail and closed with a solemn reiteration of Keith's fears. When Jake finished, she said, "I understand," and walked over to Larry and bent his fingers again.

"OW!" he roared. "I thought we had a deal!"

"Deal's off."

"Why?"

"Because you are dead asleep between your ears and an insensitive jerk to boot."

"Huh? Asleep?" Larry looked lost. "I don't understand."

Brienne slapped the back of Larry's head in the same way he had done so often to others. "How do you like that?" she asked. "This is not a sound-bite conversation, Larry. This matters and I'm serious! You will never awaken unless you stop doing the things that insults your soul—like insulting a friend. *Especially* when he is in a time of need."

"I'm sorry!" Larry pleaded. "I didn't really mean it. I've been under tremendous pressure. I'm not proud of what I've done. I—I—"

"Listen to yourself," Brienne interrupted. "I—I—I—I—I! Even your apology is a self-centered rant. Confession is not wallowing away in narcissistic self-pity. Larry, can't you see that your life isn't always about you?"

****

"She's smart," observed God.

"Yeah, and that worries me," Lucifer replied. "If she keeps this up, I'm going to zing her, too."

"That wouldn't be fair."

"What's fair got to do with this? I'm just interested in winning."

"Winning isn't everything."

"That's not what Pastor Donny says. He says you love winners."

"Luce, he's on your team, not mine."

****

Larry hung his head, rubbed his aching fingers, and moved closer to the cache of beer and snacks. Tossing a can each to Kyle and Keith, he glanced toward Brienne, saying to the pair, "One thing you guys don't have to be scared of is running out of suds with me around."

They caught their beers and both gave Larry a friendly thumbs up.

Brienne quipped, "Larry, remember that a double thumbs up means three times the obligation to stop being a jerk."

Larry nodded and gave Brienne a thumbs up.

Jake said, "Brienne, I'm impressed. You always know how to cut through the bull, expose what's real, and make sense of things."

She shrugged. "I guess I have a knack for it. For me making sense out of life is like walking through a wet desert. If you can do it, you are in a dream world, then you know you have it wrong. And if you cannot do it, then you are alive and still in the real world. There, you can still attempt to figure things out."

"Have you figured things out?" Jake asked.

"Yes, some of it—I think."

Eagerly Jake made an appeal for insight that could explain his life's downturn. "Please, tell me what you know."

"I can't."

"You can't? Why not?"

"Anything I share will seem ludicrous."

"I don't get it. Ludicrous…how so?"

"The things I know will mean nothing to you unless you find them yourself. The desire to know must spring from inside; if not, you'll be as clueless as Larry."

"Can you at least give me a push or a hint at how to start?" he pleaded.

Brienne hesitated. Her face took on an expression of deep thought. She sighed, and then asked, "Why is the ocean so close to the shore?"

"What? A silly question—that's it? That's all you can give me?"

"I tried to explain—there's nothing to give."

"Ah, come on, please?" Jake begged.

Brienne grinned and rattled off a series of similarly silly questions. "What is the weight of blue? Describe the smell of time? What shape is the sky? What time is love? What color is 3 p.m.?"

"Wait—wait! Now I really don't understand!"

"You sound like Keith. Are you scared, too?"

"No!"

"Well, that's a start."

"A start? Of what?"

"The search—your search. It begins when you ask questions."

"What am I looking for?"

"I don't know. The beginning. The end. Truth. God, perhaps?"

"Yes. Maybe that. Yes, maybe God."

"Then start your search."

"Where? How do I know when it ends? How can I be certain I've really found what I am looking for? If I just ask questions—senseless ones—can I really find God?"

She replied, "The Creator, the true God, will answer all your questions—even the ones that seem to make no sense. The ones that answer silly questions."

****

"That's it!" shouted Lucifer. "You can't fool me. She's another ringer!"

"Not so," God answered.

"Up 'til now, no one has shown any real interest in you."

"I made them in my image. Why wouldn't they think about me?"

"Because I've taught them not to!"

"How'd that come about?"

"Come on, you know."

"Yes, but I like to hear it from you."

"Okay, okay. It's like this. First, I challenge any message attributed to you. Second, if anyone believes your words, I just change them and cook up my version."

"You lie to them, right?"

"Sure, I do—I lie all the time. I've even been called the Father of All Lies. Now, back to my list... Third, I plant doubt by asking, 'Did God really mean what he said?' Fourth, I get them to question your basic level of concern with, "The worldwide death rate is two people per second. Does God really care about that fact?"

"Luce, you do not miss a beat."

"That's not all. Fifth and finally, I promise that I'll make them more like you...being immortal is really big now."

"That's quite a program. What do you do when it's not going your way?"

"Easy. I lie some more and promise them whatever their hearts desire."

"Luce, you are really something."

"You made them in your image, but they are not you—they are weak. I help their egos grow like mine did, and I use their poor choices to lead them to me through their desires. The key is to change people outside of their awareness, and to get them to do my bidding without knowing."

"They know not what they do?"

"Yes. Oh, yes!"

God frowned and asked, "In this particular instance, *what will you do?*"

"I'll double down on the basic fact that humans are slaves to the elemental spirits of the universe."

"Simple temptation?"

"Yes. I'll use it to kill off that meddling woman's influence on my target by tempting her ego. She'll be out of the picture in no time."

****

At the end of the day, Jake had sold almost all of the items he had offered in the sale. Larry, Keith, Kyle, and Jason left as a group amid a swirl of good cheer and high fives. They astutely sensed that a closer bond could develop between Jake and Brienne, or so they thought. The quartet, and especially Jake, would soon find out otherwise.

Brienne had spent much of the day getting and responding to work-related messages. Her final words to Jake were indeed final. "Jake, I'd like to tell you something," she said with a slight tremor. "I am conflicted by the events causing your loss. I confess that on one side I saw it as an opportunity for me to finally express how much I admire you, and that in light of your changed marital status perhaps things could develop personally for us."

Upon hearing her words everything about Jake brightened, but not for long. The direction of her comments took an abrupt one-eighty.

With no joy she said, "I...I...believe...no, I am certain that our potential is not very good."

Jake looked puzzled. "Brienne, what are you saying?"

She donned a troubled face and told him, "You see, it's this way—all the back and forth today on the phone was concerning an unexpected once-in-a-lifetime career move." Sadly, she added, "I just cannot pass up this opportunity. Jake, I'm leaving—for good."

Brienne's news assaulted his fragile spirit. Although never expressed, Jake's feelings for his dear friend were the origin and resting place of his hopes for a new life. Jake knew Bienne always told the truth; now he heard it in her voice and realized that what he hoped for would never be. The seed that was his hope for a new future was not meant to flourish.

Jake slumped as if shot through the heart. His inner core moaned, *Why has God let this happen to me?*

****

"She is leaving him for a better lifestyle!" chuckled Lucifer. "He's almost mine!"

"I must admit that you are the best at what you do," God said, weeping. When we hurt, so does God.

#6

A long time later, Scotty, an elderly recluse from the neighborhood, quietly placed himself on the porch next to an almost comatose Jake. In a voice seldom heard, he stated, "They say depression can be fatal."

In a faint monotone, Jake asked, "Who's *they*?"

"*They* are all the neighbors watching you wither these past months. Since the yard sale, *they* say you have hardly moved from that chair. They have been watching your decline. They won't help. They just watch."

"Some nice neighbors, huh?"

"Lucifer's minions, and full of that *Schadenfreude* stuff."

"So *what do you say?*" Jake asked.

"I say if you are lonely when you are by yourself, you are in bad company."

Jake winced. "Anything else?"

"Yes. You only give up your power when you think you have none. It's time for you to do something. Maybe not as grand as beginning a journey or starting upon a quest, but at least get out of that chair and give them something else to talk about."

"Scotty, I barely know you. I really have no idea who you are. Why do you keep to yourself? What are you hiding from? I can't recall if we have spoken more than a half a dozen times in all the years I've lived on this block. Why on earth are you here talking to me now?"

"Three reasons—the first is about coincidences."

"Coincidences?"

"Yes. God's way of revealing he is active in our lives."

"Really?" Jake asked.

"Yes, it's true. It's the explanation for 'the hand of God' thing people believe in."

"Sounds plausible. What's number two?"

"God and needs."

"Needs? What in the world does God need from me?" Jake asked.

Scotty laughed. "Now that's ego for you. It's not what he needs from you—it's what you need from him."

"Like what? What do I need?"

"To know what's wrong with you and your life. You could ask him to show you your faults. Then you can address what's wrong."

Jake said with more than a tint of indignation, "God's in charge—let him fix it!"

Scotty smiled at getting a reaction, any reaction, out of Jake, who continued.

"And if he's not in charge, it seems that *he needs me to do stuff his way* in order to appear that he is running things."

"No, no!" Scotty replied, guiding him. "I said God needs nothing from you. This is about what your fellow man needs. Your neighbor suffers from your wrongdoing just as much as you do. Likewise, he benefits from your doing good."

"Okay... Maybe, unlike my neighbors, I'll buy that I am my brother's keeper."

"It's true if you choose so, yes. The choice is yours."

Jake thought about it a while and slowly nodded his agreement. "You said there were three reasons you stopped by. What's the third one?"

"Old sins cast long shadows."

Jake looked puzzled. "You've lost me."

"This visit has three reasons, two reasons for you and one for me," Scotty explained. "The third is simply that I had to do something—to help. I couldn't let you die."

"I still don't understand. That sounds like the second one over again. You have to explain better."

"Have you ever heard of Kitty Genovese?"

****

Lucifer raised an eyebrow and squinted at God. "Gee, I wonder where he came from."

"I do work in mysterious ways," God replied, chuckling, "or maybe it's just a coincidence."

Lucifer moaned. "You and your lame jokes."

"Well, Luce, kidding aside, how do you think this contest is going?" Of course God knew how it was going, but he was being polite. "Is it time for a break?"

"Sure...sure..." replied a distracted Lucifer.

This is tougher than I imagined, Lucifer observed silently. *Maybe I've missed something. Maybe I need to devise something new. I constantly have to come up with new stuff. Half of the people easily get bored and the others quickly forget. Only a few ever catch on, and I'm amused at their naïve belief in the originality of their ideas. I'm always ahead of them on things, especially the dark stuff, yet could the people on Earth have changed since the last time we did this?*

The thought was disturbing to Lucifer. His methods were not as effective as he wanted, so he returned to "the opposing team's locker room" to refine his game plan and to check out that cute new cheerleader.

God spent the break tending to the universe.

After The Break

Lucifer was not deterred. He mused, *I'm totally committed to winning, and although this contest is not going the way I expected, I believe I have just what the doctor ordered. It's time for me to rev up the action.*

Lucifer stood near God's place in Heaven and waved his hands at Earth. "Here you go, Jake. Let's see how much God really loves you."

Lucifer had invented heart attacks for just these situations. Down on Earth, Jake grabbed his chest. The pain was excruciating. Jake's pain was pleasure for Lucifer, so he sent another jab.

"Oh, my God!" Jake wailed as he grabbed his chest a second time.

Lucifer wondered, "Why don't they ever call out my name?"

It was a rhetorical question. God did not provide Lucifer with an answer.

****

"There you are. Feeling any better?" the EMT asked.

Jake's eyes opened and he realized that he was in an ambulance with active sirens and lights.

"We thought you were a goner. I bet you thought so, too. Right?"

"No, yes, maybe…" Jake was confused. He mumbled aloud, "I wonder where I would have gone if I was a goner." He pondered more. He asked himself, *What would have happened if I didn't make it? What will happen eventually? We all die. Is there anything after death? If so, then is this just a part of a longer life? Am I something more than me—a soul, maybe? Ugh! My chest hurts even more!*

Lucifer was increasing the pain to distract Jake.

"This is bad," the EMT said. He looked worried. For many hours he would not leave Jake's side. He knew something important was happening with Jake. *Whatever happens,* he thought, *I'll stick with this patient no matter what. The doctors think they are gods, but they have forgotten that God is a doctor.* The EMT prayed for his patient.

Jake kept thinking deep thoughts.

In response, Lucifer kept cranking up the pain. It approached the highest level possible and was just almost unbearable. Lucifer took Jake to the edge several times, but the pain only caused Jake to go deeper into his thoughts.

"I want it to stop," Jake dreamed aloud through the pain. "I'm a soul. I'm a soul—I only happen to have a body. Where's God when I need him? Has he abandoned me? I want this to end. I'll do anything for it to end."

For a moment Lucifer thought, *Now, I got 'em.* But he did not.

From the farthest recess of Jake's memory, an ancient verse cycled through his mind: *Thou he slay me, yet I trust in God.*

Immediately the EMT said, "He's going to make it!"

Looking at the scene beneath, Lucifer saw that God was holding Jake's hand. In spite of the pain, through everything Lucifer threw at him, Jake could feel God touching him. Lucifer had invented pain, hoping it would cloud people's vision. God used the pain and suffering as a means for people to understand and seek him. Whenever Lucifer invented something, God had a remedy.

Lucifer noticed a bead of sweat on God's brow. Lucifer whined, "The Boss never sweated for me!" But God indeed had sweated for him; Lucifer was always too busy scheming and complaining to notice.

Lucifer was jealous. He had invented jealousy to manipulate people and to cause confusion in relationships. It worked well on people. But for Lucifer, jealousy did not work as intended—it did not feel good. Nothing

Lucifer invented ever performed as well as advertised. When God wished to punish us, he let us believe advertising.

"I haven't lost him," Lucifer persisted. "I just need a little more time." In a burst of anger and desperate creativity, he decided to "play God." He took a move from the Boss's playbook and gave Jake a gift—a full recovery laced with temporary memory loss. "He'll fit into the world now. He'll still be mine."

Time passed.

A year out of the hospital and Jake's analysis of his situation was that "things aren't so bad." The kids were towing the line; the alimony disappeared when Jen-Jen dumped Mr. BMW for a better lifestyle and married the judge. Jake had even found a new and much better job. *Life is good*, Jake reflected.

Lucifer had arranged everything. He dropped Jake's golf handicap by four strokes, and if things continued on course at work, it was rumored that Jake would be the manager of the new "pine-scented, embossed, mega-roll project" being developed at the new toilet-paper factory where he now worked. *Yes, life is very good*, thought Jake. A private parking space was even in his future.

Lucifer mused, *Give them their hearts' desires—just give them what they want—that's all it takes.* Lucifer invented the practice of killing someone with kindness. It was a bad attempt at a paradox.

Although Jake was enjoying the fruits of a better *here and now*, he occasionally wondered about the meaning of life, God, and his relationship with him. When Jake attempted to discuss the topic with people they just changed the subject, or even flatly told him that they did not need God. Lucifer was so much in the picture that they could not look past his works to see God. On Earth life was one big party. The music was loud—so loud that people could not hear God whisper to them.

God, being God, just watched and patiently waited.

Lucifer was worried by God's inactivity, and it made him all the more frenzied in his production of material bounty to distract Jake.

Since establishing his own shop, Lucifer worked harder than he had ever worked for God. His work was never done—he invented, big and small, all forms of negative and repellant stuff, like belching, TV commercials, and inflation. He passed on to Earth all his work-related anxieties—worries about late fees when paying invoices, pensions, and the like. Lucifer also invented the idea of taxes and the surcharge. He devised the practical joke, which was neither practical nor funny. In fact, all humor based on hurting or ridiculing someone was a Lucifer thing.

Lucifer never let up.

Neither did God.

Instead of practical jokes, God played patty cake with sick kids while putting the finishing touches on casual Fridays and paid vacations.

God took pleasure in fun things such as slow dancing, friendship, root beer floats, and *Looney Tunes*. God always smiled when he thought of wind chimes, butterflies, peanut butter, and Guy Kibbe eggs. God liked to share all his good stuff with everyone. Simple things were his favorites, like an egg fried in the center of a holed-out slice of bread. God was particularly pleased with his invention of the trickle-down theory, and used it to share his love instead of money.

Lucifer was so busy being bad that he did not notice that God had invented something for him. After Lucifer had quit working for him and left Heaven, God invented the idea of homecomings to lure Lucifer back into the light for good.

****

Jake was a finite being, and as he aged he became increasingly aware of and concerned about time, specifically how much he had left. Soon it was late in Jake's life and he started to wonder more about its meaning, especially God's role in his own life. The tardiness of Jake's concern did not offend God—he'd take it whenever Jake was ready.

God was patient. Lucifer was not.

Therefore, Lucifer set about emphasizing the dwindling remainder of Jake's time on Earth. Lucifer had invented the two-minute warning and sudden-death playoffs to increase the drama about the End. God preferred extra innings and the sacrifice at bat, which God had only used on one memorable occasion as a player-coach. Lucifer never understood the strategy of self-sacrifice. It was his loss.

Recognizing that his time was growing short, Jake started communicating with God more often. Jake did not consider what he did as praying. God did not mind—he listened anyway. At times Jake swore that he heard God reply to his non-prayers. One time, Jake mused aloud, "I have had a lifelong nostalgia for a home I've never seen." Keith-like, he added, "I don't understand."

In response, Jake heard from God. "It is more important to yearn for home than to understand."

Jake considered the predominately one-way dialogue as "conversations with the infinite." God was okay with that, too. God was very understanding and a good listener. After all he is God. What did you expect?

Although mostly one-sided, there were times when Jake had some really great exchanges with God. It was as if God was his friend. Jake liked having a friend looking out for him. When God was not available (lots of other people needed attention, too), God assigned an assistant to keep an eye on Jake's situation. God invented guardian angels as his pinch-hitters just to protect people.

Sub rule 3a, paragraph 7 of the contest rules stated that pinch-hitters were allowed, so a guardian angel "ran interference" on everything Lucifer zinged at Jake. It was a game changer and Lucifer soon fell behind, and was more so each day. All in all, the trend line indicated that he was losing. Lucifer desperately wanted to win. He'd even cheat, but that would be very difficult because God saw and knew everything.

That's God.

When people had faith, Lucifer's tactics were ineffective. In desperation, Lucifer attempted to fill Jake with doubt. Lucifer had invented doubt as a countermeasure to faith. Doubt kept Lucifer in the game, but sometimes the doubt thing backfired. For some peculiar reason doubt could make faith stronger. Lucifer surmised that somehow God was behind the whole faith-rising-forth-out-of-doubt thing. It was a paradox.

Lucifer was not pleased when he heard Jake telling a coworker about his faith.

"I believe that if I believe, all will be well," Jake espoused. When pushed for more, or in defense of his new and often unpopular beliefs, Jake would simply shrug his shoulders and say, "As an ordinary man, I know I have no claim to the Truth, but I do know one thing—there is a God, and that I am not him."

Lucifer's frustration with Jake grew to the point of exploding. "Darn it!" Lucifer exclaimed to God. "He won't give up on you! Right now I'd like to shower him with dog poop, and not just as a joke, but as a constant shower of excrement to express how I feel!"

Despite Lucifer's wrath, Jake's faith increased, and as it increased his prayers became more frequent. So did the return messages. Finally, Jake actually had a long conversation with God when he was very sick and near the End. Some people called it the process of dying, or meeting your maker. Jake felt like he was going home.

Jake had many questions. Naturally, God had answers.

****

Jake addressed God. "Is it you?"

"Oh, yes. I am God—the one who created you."

"I need to ask why you made me capable of living without you, yet you want me to draw ever nearer to you. Why?"

"Because I need and seek *your* love."

"I do not understand. I was told you needed nothing from me."

"People get things wrong about me all the time. I made you in my image. Like seeks like, and I *am* love."

"I get it." Jake was comforted.

They sat in silence for a moment. Or was it an eternity?

Finally, Jake asked, "You made all things, right?"

"Indeed. I am the Creator."

"Why did you create Evil?"

"I didn't."

"But it does exist," Jake asserted.

"Yes and no."

Jake was uncertain. "Now, I really don't understand."

"Let me explain," God said. "People think that dark is the opposite of light, but they are wrong. If that were true, light and darkness would merely be two sides of one thing. Dark is not the opposite of light—*it is the absence of light*. And so it is with Evil. The absence of me is Evil—a state of being without me."

"How did it come about?"

"Choice—some of my creations chose to live without me."

"So evil is only a matter of choice?"

"Yes—bad choice. Or a number of bad choices," God explained.

"But choice, nonetheless?"

"Yes. By exercising the free will I gave them, some of the beings I love so much chose badly."

"Why did you not stop them?"

"If I did, then what they did would not be choice. It's a paradox. Conscious beings require choice. Life without choice is not life, and if they cannot say 'no,' then 'yes' means nothing. Although I knew they would eventually choose wrongly and reside in Evil, in my infinite patience, I know that they can again choose to be with me."

"So we, not you, are responsible for all the evil things?"

"There is God and Not God."

"I take that as a 'yes.'"

With a smile God replied, "That is your choice."

"I understand," Jake said. He smiled widely and then asked, "What is the best way to choose?"

God's answer emanated affection of the deepest order. "I desire that you love all, hurt none, trust in me…and just come home."

Quietly, Jake asked, "Is it normal that I often feel so alone?"

"You are not alone. In the spiritual realm my angels and I are aware of you more than you imagine. And remember that my love is as boundless as I am."

"I do wrong things even when I'm trying my hardest not to. Do you still love me—even when I screw up?"

"Oh, yes—even then."

"So when things happened in my life—the bad and the good—you were just letting me be me?

"Yes...but not always. At times, I did allow other forces to influence you."

"I don't understand."

"Just know that you are my favorite, yet I love each of my children equally, individually, and infinitely.

"Huh?"

"Trust me, it's a paradox based upon infinite love."

Jake felt God's love as never before. His eyes swelled with tears as he pleaded, "Oh please, forgive my sins; their weight breaks my heart."

"A broken heart is stronger when it mends, and your coming home will repair your heart's aching. In fact, it will fix everything. I love you despite sin, and I yearn for you to pass through it on your way home. You have made tremendous progress. Most people want to ignore me and go their own way—not to be known as sinners. It is their ego. It owns the sin, not them. When an ego dies it makes room for all the love I send."

Jake felt good to the deepest part of his being and remained silent for a long time. He then said, "Some time ago, a friend nudged me toward you. Her method included some whimsical questions and riddles."

"I like those sort of things. I bet you are going to ask me one."

"Yes. One stuck in my mind and I must know if it was a trick or if there is something to it."

"Ask away!"

With the slightest grin, Jake asked, "Why is the ocean so close to the shore?"

God told Jake, "That's easy. You choose to see the ocean and the shore as two separate items when they are actually two parts of the same thing. I created all things entwined. It has many names—oneness, singularity, unity, and communion. Your viewpoint hides the answer."

"Now I understand—it's consciousness, paradox, and choice. There is God and not God—being is with you or without you—in unity or the void. Which makes you...everything?"

"Yes. I explain it by saying, 'I am the I am.'"

****

"I hate this," muttered Lucifer. "For the sake of pleasure people will do the most appalling things, but when they start praying it can lead to chummy Q-and-A get-togethers like this one. Whenever people ask me to answer their deepest spiritual questions, I just give them material answers—or I simply lie. This doesn't look good for me."

God addressed his former number two. "What do you say, Luce? Had enough?"

"Yeah, yeah—I quit," Lucifer replied. You win—I'll cry, 'Uncle.'" With sarcasm, he yelled, "Uncle—Uncle—Uncle!"

"I prefer, Father."

"Okay, whatever! You won—isn't that enough?" Lucifer just wanted to collect his marbles and leave. As you might expect, Lucifer was a sore loser. What irked him most was the fact that God was such a good winner. "You are so magnanimous, and so kind," razzed Lucifer.

God never razzed a loser. After all, he was God. He recognized that sarcasm often masked pain. He also recognized a being in need.

"Luce, in this contest, did you learn anything?" God asked. God never missed an opportunity to display a teaching point, open a door, or bind a wound.

"Yes."

"And?"

"You're still in charge."

"And?"

"For some reason you love them regardless of what they do. You even love them when I get them to do evil stuff, some of which are really disgusting and rotten."

"Good—you did learn something! And you really tried—even though it was to defeat me."

Lucifer replied sarcastically, "Well, that's a big Nothing Burger with Whoop-de-do sauce."

"Don't take it so hard," God said. "You know, if you tried as much at being good as you do at being bad, everything would be fine." God did not want Lucifer to go away feeling dejected, so he complimented even his misguided effort. God was sensitive to feelings. "One day, someone will write another story about all of this. And then another someone will read it and understand."

"Understand what?" asked Lucifer.

"Everything. The imperfection and perfection of life—existence itself."

"You would know," Lucifer said, his reply layered with jealousy.

"I know that if something is possible it will happen. Infinite time, paired with infinite choice, steeped in infinite patience will make every wish to come true."

"What wish did you ever need to have come true? You are always so perfect."

"Yes, I am."

"It doesn't seem fair—you being God, perfect all the time, and me being just...just..."

"Just what?"

"Not God."

"Luce, when you come home, you will understand, and remember."

"Remember what?"

"The way it was before you chose to leave me."

"It was your decision to give me a choice. That I do remember."

"I had to give you a choice. Without it you would have just been a glorified robot. You don't want to be a robot, do you?"

"No, I guess not," Lucifer said with a shrug. Since leaving Heaven, Lucifer missed God's love. God knew that. And although Luce missed the love, he hated to admit it. God knew that, too. So God extended an invitation.

"Luce, just come see me without an agenda—no games—no snooping. Would you do that?" God asked.

Lucifer thought about it. "I don't know, maybe..."

"Luce, I'm always here for you. I've got plenty of time. As a matter of fact, I have all the time there is."

The remark reminded Lucifer about the Father Time joke and he perked up. "Boss?"

"Yes, Luce?"

"Do you love me as much as you love them?"

God saw this one coming. God was very perceptive and nice—full of love.

Lucifer's question was one God wanted to answer for a very long time. "Yes, Luce. Of course I love you as much as I love them."

"That's swell. That's really swell."

"It's my nature."

"I know. That's another thing I've learned," Lucifer replied. He wanted to profess his desire for reconciliation, but after everything that had happened, it was difficult. His ego, shored up by an eternity of bad choices, stopped him. As Lucifer turned to leave, God stopped him.

"Luce..."

"Yes?"

"Watch out, you are about to step on something unpleasant."

Lucifer looked down and quickly sidestepped some of his favorite invention. He looked up to God, flashed a smile filled with pent-up affection, and said, "By warning me, you just missed an opportunity at one of the funniest jokes ever."

With firmness, God said, "Existence is not a joke. From the moment you left me, your rebellious and tortuous ways have ruined many souls, yet I love you. But do not mistake my love for weakness."

Lucifer replied softly, "Never." Waiting a moment, he asked, "Is it okay—I mean really okay—if I stop in again?"

God answered, "No matter how improbable the possibility, I will wait for your return."

"That's good. I needed to hear that," Lucifer said as he shuffled into shadows black as grief.

God felt Lucifer's longing as if it were his own. Lovingly, he said, "Luce, there is no reason for you not to come home."

From within the dark, Lucifer murmured, "Maybe…maybe…later."

God spoke into the darkness. "Remember, I am infinite love."

And the Universe shouted, "Amen!"

Author's Comments

This story is an account of God and Lucifer competing for one soul—maybe mine, and perhaps yours, too. I offer it as a starting place for examining the role of choice, good versus evil, and the sovereign power of God's love for his creations.

Storytelling is the age-old means to make sense of that which cannot be fully understood. By updating the ancient story of Job, the oldest biblical book, I wish to examine things in the modern world that I know, believe, desire, and yet do not fully understand.

I believe that each of us is Job. As life and his relationship with God is with Jake—it is also for each of us. Similar to Jake, I believe that if I believe all will be well. I also believe that redemption and rest is to be found in Heaven. Additionally, I know there is a God and I am not him. Such is the condition of a finite being contemplating the infinite. As explained two centuries ago by Novalis, my yearning for the home I have never seen resides in all of God's creations and will end upon returning to "Father's House."

As said in the original version of Job's story, God bandages the wounds he makes and our healing comes in unity with him.